SHARING PLASTIC

blake nemec

the operating system c. 2018

SHORING PLASTIC

ISBN 978-1-946031-20-4
Library of Congress Control Number 2017918837

This text was set in V5 Prophit, Futura, Minion, Franchise, and OCR-A Standard. Books from The Operating System are distributed to the trade by SPD, with ePub and POD via Ingram.

It was edited and designed by Lynne DeSilva-Johnson, with assistance from Jay Besemer.

Illustrations by Blake Nemec, except for those appearing on pp 6, 21 & 51, which were created for this book by Pascal Emmer. Photos on pgs 16 & 18 taken by Sarolta Jane Vay.

the operating system
141 Spencer Street #203
Brooklyn, NY 11205
www.theoperatingsystem.org
operator@theoperatingsystem.org

SHARING PLASTIC

blake nemec

The author wanted to reproduce the warmth that is released by the passionate friction of [workers'] tongues, the verbal steam of their communal bath.

-Dubravka Ugresic

This book is dedicated to Sequoia, Ruby and my other sisters and brothers we lost from fatal hate violences against them as unprotected workers; I remember all that was in the air when we talked.

contents

BANTER

STAMMER

o

POETICS AND PROCESS

BANTER

Our fingers note tight nerves in the cellist's body, we sashay over
skin, slide down the trick's stomach, roundness and thighs in hot
water, blush like Freestone
fruit, unheard in concert halls where string players bend
over wood. Here us hookers giddily arch
into the musician, plucking
her arms, neck and legs as we fill
her up.

Sherry and I then bounce across the Berkeley sidewalk and slip our hot tub soaked
bodies into a taxi. Our spandex packed thighs and backs sit on the worn seats.
    -Scheherazade, on San Pablo and 54th St. please.

-She was really hot, I say looking out the window, smiling. *Is it all there?* I ask about
the money. *-I know what a wailer—really great,* Sherry says laughing while counting
twenty-dollar bills. *Yeah, it's all here and a $150 tip! -Would you have done it for free?
-I don't know—our paths wouldn't ever cross. -But if? -If she's that loud in public, yeah
if she always sounds like that, man, hell yeah, it's really -grounding? -Yeah, like when
you can hear someone reaching out for everything in the room -it's like*

sun, as the taxi rushes past a card club and recycle store, a Goodwill and Ethiopian
restaurant; Sunday crowds walk the sidewalks as Sherry and I let our heads lay back
against the seat as San Pablo Avenue drifts
by any other name
would smell like arrival
of a large self where plastic flowers sit well in our hair and the smooth leather
soles of our heels run all the way to the toes. Bright teal
awnings appear for rain or a selfie back
drop my jaw from every night's clenching over the wall's mold over the disappearing
bees over the parlor raids over California's
drought over our marriage licenses existing non
existing over the failure of Prop K over the
rainbow, I am.

everything we bounce is matter

We open our brooms, our backs
brace every agenda about us with microphones
whose cables run to our team
stirs our cauldron, elixirs are sound
spots, bubbling
between

glad trash
bags of energizer
batteries, balls
of tide
laundry soap, the silky stuff for heads
and shoulders. Hot dam
dental dams for angel
soft paper a win
decks of kleenex
tissues and an ivory shower
gel. jell-o pudding
popsicles and pop
tarts. Her
she's bar none. Gun
oil. Healthy
vibes. Astro
glide. Clean
well the bounty, full
on, to
ward off those
round
about
houses, those work
rooms and benches, those band-shells where our voices of products
meet and bend into an other score those electric opals.

Their lockers draped long lines of head: curly red, stringy brown,
platinum hair: pinned to a removable cap. Their locker

mirrors reflected different silhouettes the boys packaged to pay
rent, a line, a rent boy, in proxy a rent boy

bucking and clanging inside frames reinvented
hair falling, down the right and left

cheeks, moving across rulers for breasts, hips and penis. Billy and Andy were
pushing those gauges around. Always rearranging their bodies

of work. -*When's your next session? -At 5: golden shower; it'll only take him 15, I've got 2
hours to waste.* As they sat in the dungeon together, Andy is teeth playing with Billy's
skin. White bone over

camel tone. Beaver with wood catching the flow.
-*Not so hard!* Billy snapped. -*I thought you were flirting.* Andy held

Billy's flesh in his mouth, the phones starting to ring. -*I was
but...* He took Andy's dirty blond
hair in his palm, clutched a bit then lifted his head

up, Andy's mouth agape.
-*but don't bruise my rent.*

Andy horse laughs away to the phones. -*Damiens place,
how can we serve you? Hi John, you're running late?, I'll let your boy*

know, Billy
stood up,

slapped his shins awake, pulled a red wig off the door. -*I always wanted to be
Raggedy Ann,* he stood in front of the mirror in his tightie whities, adjusting
the hair. -*It takes*

a lot of money to look that cheap. -O Dolly O O Dolly, O O O looking for
my Dolly. -It's My Donna. -Right, I know, the Hair one. Andy said behind Billy's
body as he pulled her hair
out to the side so she looked like Daryl Hannah. –But I was talking your Parton
quote, hey that looks cool: redheaded Kate Moss with a little
willy, put your arms on my hips,

she told the boy who had her back. Andy's pasty hands sat on Billy's hips.
-Oh you got that? -I've been a Dolly fan longer than you have. -I meant the Hair.

-Hair here, hair there. -You have a hairy minded
pink, bare bear

she finished. Another song, pointed
to Andy's Chest. Their torsos

swooshed past each other's
images, but bent towards each other's mouths lipping off, waves between.

-look at all their trash in only one week -yeah you got bags from both
kitchens? -uh-huh -and bathrooms? -yeah a lot of
waste from one run -this family -and we gotta take care of
these people -broken printers -soiled diapers -formula
packets -energy drinks -can't understand it all we're looking at
-perfume and cologne -samplers -broken
toys -xbox players -luncheables -surveillance cameras -busted screens and toddler
gates -look at them, fix the
skin pads -tame your curling irons -yea lift your
highlights -whiten your teeth
tape -keep your elasticity cream
-keep your
volume -yea you know we're tryin' -we
came -look at this -mm what's that? -like a speaker -for what an ant
farm? -right, it's small enough -and not attached to
cables -or an outlet so how's it
work? -cordless?

The maids stared at the small but heavy yellow speaker box that had some syrupy
waste dripping off one of its sides as it sat under the care products at the bottom of
one of the garbage bags.

In our walkway, alley, hallway or theater apron, we share one another's shakes, back and forth. Trading words for direction, picking up coins to scratch off lottery card bingo, we should not pay to be, beehives. Caked mascara. Sliding nylons over shins. Or packing our jeans, ready-making our chatter with one another could cost us our job and all our cards you thought we hid under the table.

mirror-held portal
trap-door law circuses
face bodies coined as paper

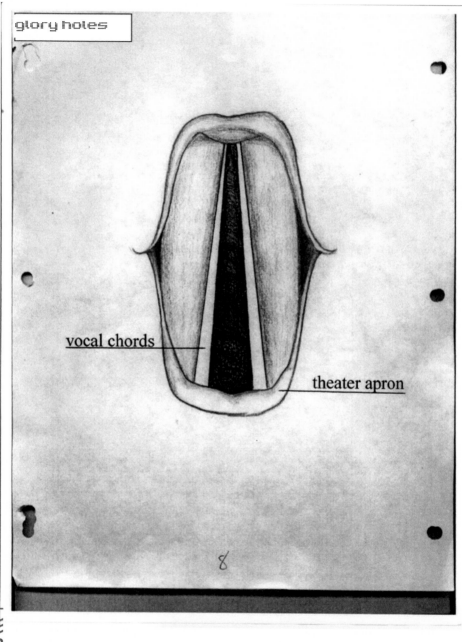

vocal chords

theater apron

8

They figure the bachelors. 5 kitty shots, 4 edible panties and 3 taffy garter belts = double the living wage for the team. Kerry reapplies a layer, cherry lipstick, before responding to her security guard's question about what they'd make from the party. *-I gotta make my base before security, before yours.* -Possible. Troy asks the dancer with un-lilted word. *-If they give beyond their means -I mean you gotta factor me,* he stands. South San Francisco salt holds inequalities the stripper and her guard didn't assay. Simplify the equation. If a line divides fixed wages the parts are greater than the sum. *-How drunk's the bachelor? -Wasted,* the dancer sees. *-Hold my hand—we'll turn the salt into solution,* he calculates. The guard fills a bucket with water and the team returns to the inebriated, flooding each hungry pocket, so their Powerballs, singles and Dunkin' Donut coupons float around in their pant holes. The bills swim out and flap their jaws about sharing pockets with white grain.

Cash money shifts land
scapes. Half of a dozen tomato vines + sidewalk stalks
coin monies, tax free hand to
hand movement. Shifting
between the Chihuahuan desert and ½ Moon
Bay. Skills juggled between workers began with hand-
shakes, open
contracts through word of mouth
2 mouth signposts.

Both hands slid over the bed cover, feeling each other's pull. *-That's a long time and the Bronos know you have car trouble? -Yeah their solution was another shift. -How generous of them,* Troy stiffly said like a Pez doll, trying hard to give Graciella something but he was rigid, with himself and the bed's wrinkles. Graciella kept on, finding signs of the owner's night-time tossing that she took care to smooth over. Her hands knew erasure made beds.

-You feel comfortable asking for more? -You missed it, she said, and walked in front of Troy to show him, swatting the ruffle like a fly. She erased further kinks, tinier ones than before, ones he couldn't straighten because he didn't see. *-Let's get the pillows,* she walked towards the stack on the Tuscany chair.

Then hundreds of pillows towered in her arms and on her shoulders as she walked back to the bed. One by one she shifted her weight to allow their graceful landing. They started lapsing down into place and onto the comforter, her aware of their filling and ruffles. When the bed was covered it was time to straighten the cases. She reached under them and pulled, the pillows leaned against one another like dominos mid-fall. He tried to follow but his jumpy movements bumped pillows off the bed instead. *-Pull smooth,* she said, her hands guiding the pillow cases. *-How's that?* He yanked at their lining.

-You're rough and too quick: keep moving gracefully as you work. He obeyed and entered the mound but made all her pillow work tumble to the right. *-No!* She taught, *no, Mr. Brono won't have it—we have to do it over.*

-It's just pillows, he said. Graciella's face soured and her body stiffened. *-Pillows are my paycheck,* and she ran to take care of his mistakes. He wanted to know how long she'd been there as he smoothed the peripheral wrinkles, not lifting anything. *-You have to get the underneath creases,* she continued. He stepped over to her side of the bed, *-you've been here awhile huh? -Six years,* she said, it *is what I have it's just that-*

He leaned towards her, - *yes? It's just what?* She stepped away from him, *-listen you can't even make a bed. I see—I hear what you're saying, but you can't even make the bed.*

She slid her hands over the bedspread, all those pillows on top of her arms. First, she gathered and supported the left side then the right until they again, for that moment, stood.

Violette shook the largest rug from the top of the stairs while Tatja batted it with a broom.

-*Wait, hold it still so I can get it...* Tatja pleaded. -*Just a shake over here...*Violetta quipped. -*Well I can't do my job when it's flyin' everywhere.. -just a sec and you can strike.. -gonna be hard when it's up in the.... -there. Give it your best shot! Come... -it's still moving, why's it...? -I'm not shifting it HEY watch that stick you're hitting my leg... -no, that's just the weight of this thing, not the broom.. -too hard to just be carpet. -Hold steady this thing got filthy just since last week I gotta get at the binding.. -ouch—shit you hit me again... -not me it's the material, hey, let's see it.. -watch where you swing, damn. -ok I'm looking, put it... -don't hit again.. -put it... -yes I won't hit.. -promise? -Put it... -promise? -We gotta get the job... -I'm not until you.. -yea. -yea? -Yea... -kay, come.*

Talk is rope. Strands gliding
over rows of chatting lip, and back
bones, these hairy tongues are *Close
to the Knives* of the *Thief's
Journal.* Ducking below bands of blond
hair. Black, brown, or red
umbrellas whose forms refract the next
lock and form a shawl, thousands
of scarves warm necks with the *City
of Night, Unrepentant
Whore,* these braids arc towards the ears, the sound
organs and hair lines—ancestral, so it can be followed, heads hold volume, a mass
organized. Hands grab
to form another rope. Climb up
reigns because chords feel
good in the palm.

Candle wicks are for fire
before they're lit, they're holding waves
waiting to crack into flame.

Yanking one thread for heat may spark
rituals of braiding. Light
rises off
fire like a fast flame, lighting
many twisted
wicks
beams
through scabs, union
busters and those pimping bodies as coins.

Place comb teeth on the heads and the roots, to source. You'll be *Pulling
Taffy* hearing *Rent Girl[s].* These talkers are good braid.

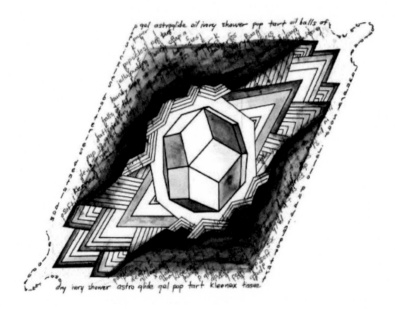

gal astroglide oil ivory shower pop tart oil balls of

dry ivory shower astro glide gal pop tart kleenex tissue

The South San Francisco trailer park held workers. A cashier watched football, a trucker moved a soap bar across his back, a call center operator bent over a bathtub—scrubbing fiberglass while a stripper was getting blown. A 49ers game sounded out of a couple of trailers next to the one my friend turned a trick in. I rolled the window down, taking in the scent of Dune grass; the evening air was cool compared to the heat of that October day. I sat back in the car seat to enjoy an hour of being on call. At 5'3, 130 lbs I was security-like, a trip-wire. If something went down I could set off a series of actions to get my friend out of danger.

Workers dress up as Emma, Eddie or Betty super
sense, their identities somersaulting to the
top and bottom of a relation: needs for self push back
bending auras, stretch edges so the I lines of service are
skirts or shorts. Never flesh or teeth,
stay honey inside our mouths. Ties sway off
the right or left shoulder. We are

sucking KOOLS real fast after quitting, we sing "We're On a Road To Nowhere," loud. In a Chevy Corvette we are singing with the windows down, in an Albertson's parking lot. We are not on Hwy 66 or "On The Road;" we're off Interstate 10, where Mexico, New Mexico and Texas kiss. Then in aisle 1, where the bread has gone up to 5 dollars. 5 dollars for white bread is a spongy rip-off I must own as part of my product, here in El Paso, where breakfast, lunch and dinner are served with tortillas. And I've found my head

happens down on Texas Avenue, young
men step into tall trucks, ride
around the block. Mouths
shift tones, volume and pitch
poems to editor lips, pitch
yeses across streets, other babes sigh
"Oh" back at their boys catch
mittens come in latex and nitrile
covers our dicks. Our faces you see

-*Denny!* Illona hollered my name from inside the trailer. I got her out of there faster than the muscle head suspected a little guy could pull a chubby queen out from behind him. -*I'm sure she did her job,* I told him in response to his anger over their session. Illona and I were both back inside her car trying to leave, and locate safe. The John's body went up against our tailgate, a knife in his hand. Our small bodies held heat of impending violence in our chests. He held a cell phone while telling us the lies he'd tell the cops so we would imagine our builds behind bars. I held up my own phone yelling up some stories myself so stripper John could accept he was not the only tall tale teller there. I could see him in the rearview mirror, his body against the tailgate and tire, so we couldn't bounce out of there. -*He's got a knife,* I said. -*Fuck, it's not worth it,* she said knowing our threats would never even out she jumped out and gave him some coins back.

On the highways, our blood
pressures rise as we're thrown against walls,
cells fill up. Before the canals open
for people smoking trees for people giving
blowjobs or trade formerly known as medicinal
counters are turn-styles. Name them Wednesday or Mon
tana the person, unwilling to give
up hope—an accumulation of water
forms in the sky, we can read to know *All Tomorrow's Party.*

Men stand by SF's 26th and Florida stop sign, ready
to work, be picked up, their bodies
washed and hair combed for the drivers. This corner's
hot, but they stand anyway. The cash money is worth the wait,
and danger. Money is waiting they imagine
their biceps will sweat in trade, as hired
hands. So help me
god, all our heels and boots share the concrete. They learn
one another's,

-how are the babies? -Sarah just lost teeth and David's needing
new shoes every day. Robbie says as he leans against the cement
wall, tooth picking his teeth. -Yours? -Just one, Vanessa, she's a talker, but not full
sentences, -just fragments, right? I remember when mine were
baby talking then boom -they're connecting
pieces? -Yeah it's like all those words they've been hearing
since day one -take a second to come together? -mm-hmm -but I get her ya know -yea
you're with her everyday yeah? -Exactly, I -listen to them a couple times and -can
imagine she's sayin' pour
more when i heard pomo -yeah abuh for table -heh mine are, you'd for
food -right baba for bottle -doogerr for
sugar -bay
pay -nee
me -nigh
my -doo
due -doo
to -eep
keep -oar
your -ace
face -heh

so many - many

-No, sex and organizing are separate, Leila said as we drank Shiraz from the Santa Rita Cellars. The winery had laid down artificial lawn and we sat on it. She told me her response to a Border Networker, *-you have to organize dating*. I thought yeah I try to weave spinach salad, locally brewed wine, and informal trade into the dialogue. If sex worker talk shrivels, I try to move my body into farmers pulling peaches, to allow her distance from my body as subject. But could I be farming in an orchard, criminalized for not being documented?

Real dirt is expensive. It costs
speakers, characters and readers, each other, gossip becomes
literature when the dirt is loam. Loam comes out of
years of feeding, so when it's held it's sticky and dark
looking at loam is looking at generations
of sand and rock and dung.

The grass of this shit isn't Kerry green but lime
shards and emerald slices. It's new
narrative each time, hard to access that
loam; it's hard to keep the soil dank on all sides.

We settle for Kerry green then. The green labeled: lawn, so it is clear and concrete for sitting on without fears of ants between one's toes.

I'm not pulling up strawberries or pulling down apples. Pulling may not be pushing into holes. Digging dirt may not be sliding hands.

On this plastic turf, we're not talking about ways we handle and pick fruit. The bowl is full and the worker who filled it is jailed, or ICEd. There's Sessions. Thoughts of those bars scare all in System D it haunts

whores. This word sits on the top of my cheek bones, yesterday's laughing skin gliding over it, because we tossed it back and forth like Ping-Pong without paddles. Together, we sat on real grass; it was green and smelled in need of water and manure. It was lime and emerald, yellow and brown. I always knew it was fingered into dirt, that's why I

went barefoot. Today I'm organizing words I used to use freely. Leila is today and she always works above the table so we are just talking on astroturf.

how's it o'er on your side uh?
-hard to put my finger onna..
-uh huh, I feel you, alotta..
-mm hmmm.. -people sayin'.. -mm mmm,
what do?-thought be the way boss.. -um, -
some said.. -uh. –others.. -oh yes well.. -
I can tell a story's there. -tell
me somethin' you ever hear of..
-of talks? yeah a lot of people
talkin' bout kinds of talk and

-k, good, so you've got someone,
so I'm not the only one -naw
naw people been talkin' bout things
since I got here -people gonna
meet -that's the idea right? that
there'll be a time outside of here
-mm hmm -ok -yeah -ok I like that
that's good to hear -good, think all will
get alot out of it. thinking
so, I imagine so. -so -so

you gonna finish that room? -oh
yea, yes I just lost track of things
ya know because of thinking of
people -right -and imagining
-I'm sure -what's gonna be -I bet
you -yea I mean I'm sorta new
here so I'm picturing -easy
-right, just thinking -exactly so
-able to talk more -that is one idea -freely -listen you

shouldn't have high expectations
-oh no, I know, I just ya know
-I mean there'll be so many kinds
of different –k –things –yeah I
imagine! –k so relax right?
Right I get it we'll wait'n see.
-yea you got it just remember
-bet it's got a long history
-an different people –yea loads
to hear? –expect great fragments ok.

-Hey—they're only ones came in? -Naw
couple from two doors down too. -Get
them recorded? -Not yet man—need
a group 'fore the walls start goin'
up. -Take 'em to the site 'morrow.
-Don't recommend it boss—without
masses, things never goin' up.
We got four from yesterday boss—
That's only ten, think -Don't have to,
guys from that sister site'll fill.

In the hall between the marble floored kitchen and the Degas lined den, Vlad and Alex talked. They spoke of their work for the Bronos and about each other. Did Alex prepare everything. Was Vlad ready to mind them at their Santa Rosa estate. First, the Bronos needed to pick up some bottles of wine at their Sonoma winery, then they had a dinner date with people from their parish. It was a two-hour drive, the dinner was at 7pm, and it was 4pm. The BMW's fluids and tires were checked; the Bronos bags were already in the car. Vlad would have to speed a bit in order to get the Bronos to the dinner appointment, but he should pay no mind as long as he sped 10 mph over. Alex warned that Mr. Brono might be upset that Obamacare destroyed people's right to quality medicine but Vlad should pay no mind to the Sir's articulated frustrations and keep his eye on the road. Did Vlad remember the road. Yes, he would drive through the Presidio to the Golden Gate bridge, then he should take the smaller county roads instead of Hwy 101 as it would allow him to stop at the Bronos winery for a dinner gift. Alex continued to confirm that Vlad didn't forget any of the Bronos preferences and listed procedures while holding up fingers for each numbered step. Vlad nodded and repeated Alex's words. He then stated how the grill worked and how they liked their meat; he remembered the light and security system and how to take care of their Bichon Frise. Vlad asked what he should do if they arrived late which would upset Mr. Brono. Alex told him they would mind so could not be late.

Where were the Bronos they asked each other. Then could hear Mrs. Brono talk on the phone about her "rentals" and how she would do her best to get the toilets repaired soon. Mr. Brono was watching an ebay auction. The grandfather clock's hands could be heard as time passed. They would need to be on the road soon. But Alex and Vlad knew they needed to mind their own business; they could not say so; they must pay mind.

fortify service stations
dignity speakers
play sonic reverences

I ran from the peephole back into the kitchen where Illona was rolling a black thigh- high up her leg. I shook my head no again and again. She pinched her face and told me to turn the trick. The John behind the door looked like Brad Pitt, held a motorcycle helmet and stood about 5'10, late twenties. He brushed a hand through his sandy blond hair and squinted into the peephole while repeating his knock and looking annoyed. The peephole showed an inglorious cock. And these toy shows were benign until the viewer was a pit, like a guy they make medium sized clothes for. Illona told me to pretend he was Judith Butler but I could only see and feel a pit. Not a black hole but an apparently benign crack a shoelace would snag on and flip you flat on your face. Hard against the concrete with shredded skin.

> turnstile this maleness
> we're switchblades not artifacts
> corridors flicker

Isis's Mary Janes tapped against the tile as she swung the dungeon's bathroom door open, *that is beyond rude! - What?* Audrey responded, running to the bathroom.

If someone is giving me a message, I do not appreciate it. They would be paying me, Isis walked over to a full-length mirror, lifted her head and approved both sides of her profile. *-I'll take care of it honey,* Audrey said after seeing the toilet pee.

Isis stood in front of the mirror and spread Jojoba butter over her arms so her black skin gleaned. *-If I wanted a golden shower, I would be paid for it.* Her body was toned and smooth. She moved to the left and right so her navy-blue skirt swayed and bent as she hummed, "Ave Maria."

-Just pee, another girl, Rhoda, quipped and adjusted her chubby thighs, packaged in rubber pants. Isis gave Rhoda an evil eye through the mirror but Rhoda didn't see it. A Lifetime Special featuring Sandra Bullock played on TV. Bullock runs after a cab where she'd left her purse. Sandra doesn't make it to the cab but instead runs into a man and they smile in mutual embarrassment, realizing an attraction, then Bullock smells her underarms while the man reaches into his bag for a business card. *-Doesn't she have some idea how she smells?* Rhoda asks the TV.

Isis inspected the buttons on her silk blouse, *-I know how I smell but you don't WANT to smell completely you, do you.* She walked long and slow to the other side of the lounge. Her gait was deliberate and accurate with a seeming rhythm to when she would look down. Heel toe--heel toe--heel, look. Heel toe--heel toe--heel, look. She walked around the lounge once, then exited.

There, in the halls of *Pandora's Box*, with high ceilings and stone walls, Isis walked her fingertips over the marble. She didn't have her next session for an hour so she strolled into the medical themed room with silver trays and a white leather patent exam table. She picked up a stethoscope then set it against her chest to hear her breath as she hummed, "Ave Maria." At first she sang softly to herself but she began to enjoy the echo so got louder. She skipped over to the stirrups and used them like a podium as she arched back and filled the room with Latin. As her voice lifted from her belly, and impregnated the exam room, her hands shook the stirrups, as if to demand the metal poles work with her.

Jostling the metal, she remembered they detach. She slowly slid each side up out of their holes and walked around the room holding them up like guns, then bent her arms and held them up to her face, liked cocked pistols.

Rhoda walked in, -*your voice!* Isis kept one of the stirrups to her face, and let the other one fall. She aimed what she held at Rhoda and shouted *BLAM!*

-*Don't shoot--ah!* Rhoda gasped as she fell to the ground. Isis walked to Rhoda laying on the floor and put one Mary Jane on her shoulder, -*Sandra Bullock doesn't look good smelling herself and neither do you.* -*You were smelling.* -*You're nasty, don't remind me.* -*It's my right.* -*To be nasty, yea, I've heard that from white girls like you.* -*Gonna take that off my shoulder?* -*How's it feel?* -*It pinches and smells like floor,* Rhoda told the black woman who looked her in the eye. -*Is it my right to make you smell it?* -*Listen, I didn't mean...*

-*No, you listen because your mother doesn't live or work here.* -*What do you mean?* Rhoda pushed the Mary Jane off her face, and sat up next to Isis's metal stirrup. She ran a finger up the shaft, the only piece connecting them both, next to that white exam table where bonbons and bondage sit over tongues and slide down the length of faces.

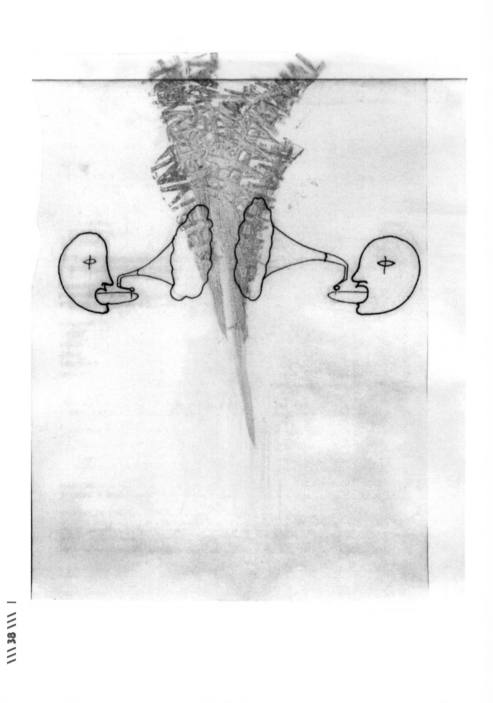

Bonnie and Craig knew the Tenderloin street blocks share a meter. She had coins and gun in her purse, but parking meters use plastic and they didn't have any for the car. -*Could pay to use someone's card?* Craig said. A guy with white earbuds dangling out of his ears neared them as he crossed Turk street. -*Him—go!* Bonnie called out. Craig skipped up to the guy. -*I'll trade you two dollars for one with your credit card.*

White earbuds squinted at him then scurried away. -*We'll be late for the film shoot,* Craig moaned, while a teenager without teeth asked for spare change. Bonnie opened her coin purse and pulled out some silver for the toothless, and a woman wearing a bluetooth started slinking by. -*We have to get the TSMs that's where all the grant money is,* BlueTooth transmitted in front of them. -*There is your girl,* Craig cheered Bonnie on, so she puffed her chest up and clicked her 70's chunks up to BlueTooth. -*Sweetheart, I am going to give you two dollars you can slide your card into the meter box for me?* -*So sorry, I'm late for wor-*

Bonnie's voice dropped real low as she showed her gun, -*share the card, girl.* BlueTooth skipped to the meter box and slid her plastic inside. So Bonnie relaxed, -*Thank you sugar, which non-profit do you work for? We'll send some "high risk" over your way.* BlueTooth's eyebrows crouched over her bulging eyes as she gazed at Bonnie and Craig; she gave them an outreach card and ran away. -*My word is good; I'll send some friends over,* Bonnie shouted as BlueTooth left. Bonnie kissed her gun, -*think she knew this is plastic?* Craig kissed Bonnie's cheek, -*by the fear in her face I don't think she knows realness.*

-Starting on the sheets? -Yea, you've got
soiled you want me to add? -Mm hmm,
got cases/spreads from the main house
I need done before night's over
-alright throw it in, cycle hasn't
started today -here we go how's
your night? -Aw you know s'hard to
get anything done when Mr. Bronos
stopping you to get your idea
on this or that, immigration
n' American Health Care Act
-mm I just say 'you don't say.'

Graciella said as she closed the triple load washer and pressed
start talks about care that cover a mandatory X-ray
Spex shouted "Identity" as they jumped in plastic bag
dresses like we can slide power
horse cans 'cross the dirty stage so aluminum sides smack against blown out speakers
that crack white noise at ends of Fifty Shades of Gray at ends of police lines up
up and away **say**
her name Sandra Bland, **say her name** Amber Monroe

-Mmm hmm, but it's hard to
say, calmly. How can we? -Collected? -I
know, I don't know he's—she's not really
asking. It's their way to sleep ya
know -at night, get sleep. You gotta
imagine being so cut off
from other -people an' other places

beamed out of their mouths lovely
service workers, as their broom hairs slid over the ground they know.

STAMMER

3 ARRESTED IN VICE TRAP IN LOOP HOTEL

Three women were charged with soliciting for prostitution and a fourth woman was charged with steering patrons to prostitution yesterday after a vice raid Thursday night in the Palmer House.

WHAT WERE THE SOUNDS?

DID THEY MM HMM TO EACH OTHER? OR UNGH UH? SIGHS?

"FALLNESS"

MIDDLE

BACKNESS

FRONTNESS

WHERE WERE THEIR TONGUES?

VOICING: WHEN VOCAL CHORDS ARE PRESSED TOGETHER THEN OPENED.

The new girl jumped into the lounge asking -*what the fuck kind of parlor are you running?* She pounced onto the couch, took Courts and Criminals out of my hands and waved it around while lifting her teddy, revealing her bush. -*Pussy or palm?* she demanded in front of me as she alternated which one she advertised. 'Didn't I see the difference?' 'Didn't I know the difference?' -*Yeah*, I cleared my throat and sat up, -*the hand doesn't self-lubricate.*

-*Ha. Ha.* She didn't laugh. -*I do massage—healing—I, do them. They do not do me.* She stood up to me like I'd pimped her out. -*You told me it was a parlor over the phone*, she pulled on the front of my blazer with both of her hands. I swatted her away and looked over to the clock reading 2:30pm which meant between picking out Donna, waiting for Donna, then Donna walking out of the session, the John had been upstairs, waiting to get off, for a half hour. He might walk and that would mean a couple of things. Bad business for our house and more importantly a bad reflection on me since I was finally supervising the shift I'd waited 6 months to get.

I needed a girl up there. I dialed the other girls who were rejected in the line-up. -*Donna's changed her mind. About the work. So, one of you needs to take him.*

Donna had been sitting across from me, on her knees, but had since collapsed forward and was telling me her progression from stripper to bachelor party girl to masseuse; 'she was always in control.' Her tears were beginning to get in the way of her talking then she grabbed my hands into hers and pressed them into her puffed up and salty face. I gave her some tissue and she kept my other hand in hers, still freaked about her identity switching before her, while continuing to tell me the clear differences between our trade. I knew how New York's Article 230 divided Donna and me. It was the inverted reason to pay Columbia an exorbitant amount to study law. I went back to the phone.

-*He's been up there for a little more than a half hour.* I told the girl over the phone.
-*Cool—I'll tell her you'll take him.* -*Another girl has got 'em*, I told Donna.
-*No I'll do it*, she shot up and made her way to the mirror. She spat on the tissue I gave her and looking into the mirror, wiped the mascara smear off her cheek and pushed her bob back.
-*Keep your tongue pressed to the top of your mouth and only do positions you feel in control of* I told her. *Do you play any instruments? -Viola*, she said. -*Play him like the Viola.*

Donna blew her nose then left the room, slowly. I resentfully restacked the law books she'd tossed around the room. The door opened back up sooner than I had imagined it would and there stood Donna.

-*Don't tell me you're that good, it's only been five minutes.*
-*He wants to watch us.*
-*I'm not doing sessions today,* I walked over to the mirror and slid my hands down the sides of my suit so the pleats over my stomach popped, so my hips looked bigger as my waist looked smaller; this suit was giving me cleavage while lengthening my legs like it knew how to push me out and make me tower.

Donna straddled the arm of the couch, twirling a strand of her curly red hair, bending her head slightly down as she tilted one of her wrists to the left and right, -*I've been told I go in easy but can still fill a lady up.*

-*You're a darling Donna, but I'm in charge of—*
-*Everything, I know—it's your court,* she slipped off the couch and knelt between my legs, then stretched her arms around my thighs to grab hold of my ass.
-*Let's go,* I told her. -*I'll get another girl to watch the phones.*

-*Business first, John.* So, he put the bills on the bed and I picked them up and stuffed them into my bra. The handcuffs were there in the next second; he caught me first and when Donna came up to me in shock, he clamped her too.

Name: _____

Due Date: _MAY DAY_____

Year 10 PSYCHOLOGY CRIMINAL PROFILING

TASK
In this assignment you must choose and research a criminal and give a detailed report on his criminal record.
YOURSELF AS ^ *YOUR BODY.*

Step 1
Look at the list attached and choose a criminal that you would like to research. *YOURSELF AS* ^
Choose carefully as everyone will chose one, you will not be able to change your mind once you have decided. *THIS ONE PART OF YOU, FOREVER*

Step 2
Use various ~~resources~~ *MIRRORS* to research answers to questions below. You may use sources such as ~~websites, encyclopaedia and CD-Roms~~ and books (** Maximum of 2 ~~internet~~ ; *PHONE SELF-*
sites **) *HAND-HELDS, FULL-LENGTH AUDIO RECORDINGS* *PORTRAITS)*

QUESTIONS *WILL PASSING EVERY HIPSTER BAR IN SOHO HELP ME PASS THE BAR?*
- ~~What is criminal profiling and what is its purpose?~~
- Profile your ~~criminal~~ *YOURSELF AS*
- Discuss ~~signature behaviour~~ *POWER SUIT. IS IT NAVY BLUE OR BLACK?*
- Discuss ~~inductive versus deductive profiling~~ *WHAT IS FASHION STYLE,*
- Timeline the events for ~~the chosen criminal~~ *OF SUCCESS! HOW MANY TRICKS DO I NEED TO TURN TO PAY FOR LAW SCHOOL?*
- Assess the criminals dangerousness *BE PROFILED*
- Should your ~~criminal by a "stalker", outline the type of stalker and reasons behind your response~~ *COP RUN.*
- Other relevant information to help ~~solve the crime.~~ *YOUR BODY.*

Step 3
While you are doing the research, ~~complete the data grid on the next page.~~ *DRINK ALOT OF WATER AND GET GOOD REST.* Write your answers to the questions in **point form only**

Step 4
Use the notes in your data grid to write a rough draft of the text that you will put onto your presentation. Develop the notes into full ~~sentences~~ that are in your own words. *BODIES*

Step 5
Come up with ~~a finalised audio-visual presentation~~ *SELF-HONOR REGARDLESS OF WHAT THE RECORD SAYS.*

INSTRUCTIONS FOR THE ASSIGNMENT
- ✓ Word limit: 700 – 1,000 words
- ✓ Presentation: Visual and Written ~~(Poster/Power Point)~~ *POEMS*
- ✓ Use ~~of~~ time: 1 library lesson, 2 classroom based lessons.

for "days in april"

A many-lipped sound check, with old, duct tape or unused
mics, stoking ambers in the gut of laborers. Their

hours, bodies, babies or food on the table. Wages, contracts May
Day dreams to cut distances in English, Spanish or Mandarin. Words rebound

off the walls of the concrete room where workers gather—Oakland, April '08.
Schemes echoed around each worker cluster, meeting together

by trade. -*They told us we'd be paid in hand, next
week, next month.* -*Then they outsourced your entire team yea?*

Talk: hot tea kettles whistling
off, get off me, off key, off the heat

melts plastic ties surrounding wrists or tongues
tied. Bent around hard

wired houses. How to keep the hunted hollering
out of haunts. Out of closets and cells. The street, warehouse, or house is work

unlike home and friend. Places of service
glued to the boss. Talking

dollars and plans to smooth grievances, protests
fracking the butane of worker gossip. Water hoses

blasting people onto their ass, because of their voice
on voices rattles cages. Cacophonies

spiral up out to show each body
it's tethered to, following the sonic spate.

Safe Work Permit

VOID

Type (hot work, confined space, line break, etc.

Valid 08/08/'66 ___ 08/08/2066 ___
From M D Y time to M D Y time

Work Description: Touching people.
Throwing coffee in the face of
obstruction to justice.

Permit # 4144

location: Oakland, CA

issued to: Brooke Nemec

Jeffrey Strouth   Jeffrey Strouth
Supervisor's Signature   Print name

Work Order No.

Differences, Filed Together

<u>8.24.06 Minutes</u>
<u>Attendees</u>
Ryan, White, Nemec, Gonzalez, Israelson, McCormick,
Plotsky, Jacobson, Sanchez and Smith.

<u>Agenda: Hotel Union Sets Strike Date</u>
Attend to hotel workers; welcome sex workers; appreciate farm
workers; address day laborers

<u>Discussed</u>
Supplies undelivered to shop premises
amount to conflicts with dollars in hand, vs. coins in contract.
Health inspect
shun of place. Each hotel, soil, street higher up
negotiations on hold, 'til next meeting,
surveilled. Zoning laws zoom in, magnify the elbow
grease marking all, made to the table.

Oak formica or pine tables hold elbows
differently, some of the tables have 100 growth rings on their
surface. Contour
lines meet each knife. A conversation topic: '..interesting etching
on its back' 'yes the farmers
walked out that mark.'

The particle boards don't show same history labor and materials
ground into gray
putty, for a mold. 'Let's not talk
about it—the help is in the kitchen,' pointing out
house as home as work as amalgam identity.

Formica tables have color when newly off the shelf. Some a street
purchase some off the internet they move from sheds to porches to
living
rooms getting nicked along the way. 'Isn't this the table the ACLU
wouldn't touch?'
'Yep, IWW are the only ones care to mention-' the street

hotel-farm table's
legs different surface area.

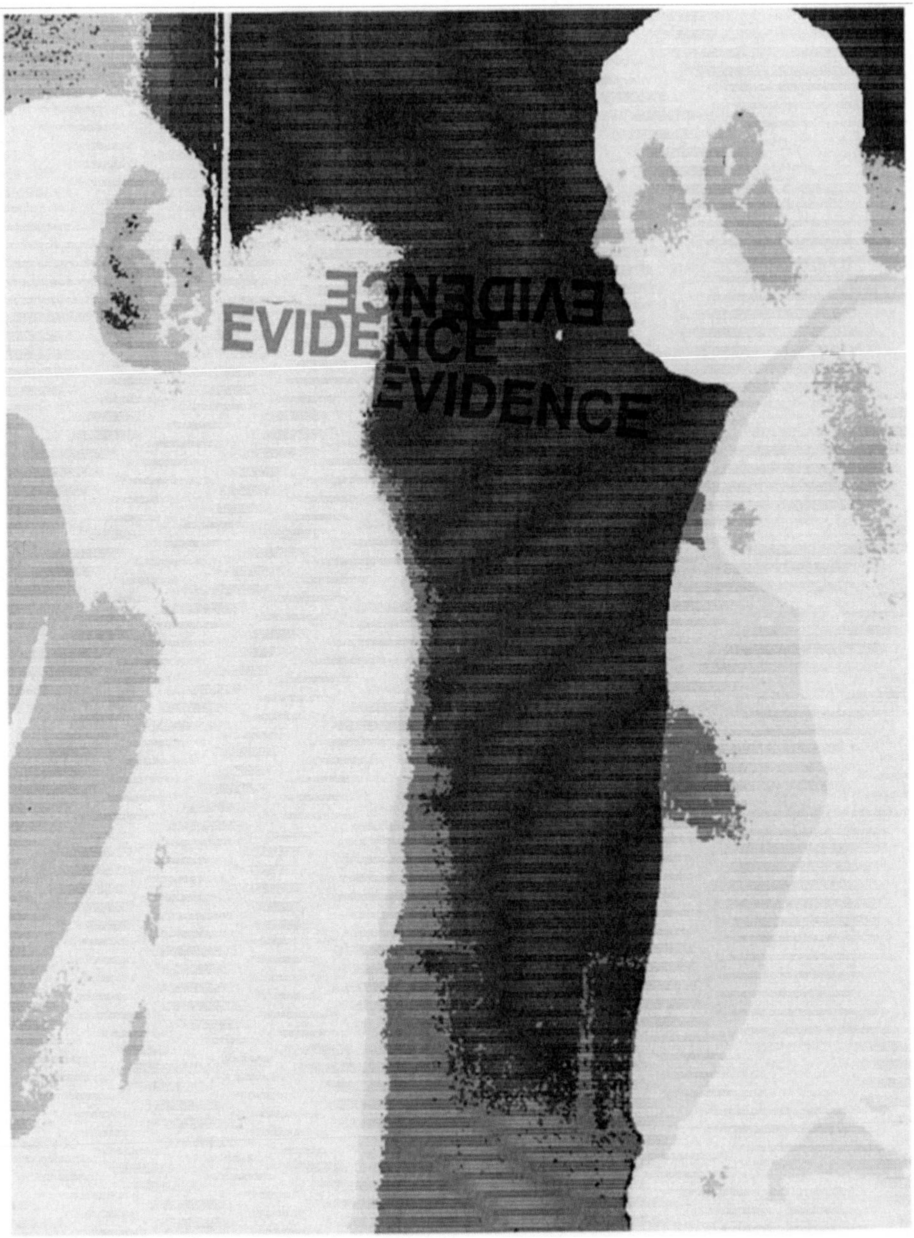
EVIDENCE
EVIDENCE

With a headache self-conscious looking at the new moon,
teachers walked down the side streets under the trees.
In their fatigue and shopping for images,
sweet portrayals to shift brown avocados into
lime fruit, they went to a farmer's market
dreaming of themselves as enumerations:
pork tripe, chicken wings, and sausage links,
dangled off the butcher's stall they saw,

what peaches and what penumbras! Whole Families shopping at
night! Aisles full of house wives, widowed fighters, cheering for the bitter melons
like Taiwan's Mrs. Guan,

they asked questions to each: who killed the pig? What price
chicken? Are you my angel?

The guides wandered beside and underneath the brilliant
cans tipping then losing in their imagination, the store detective,

they strode down the open corridor together in a
solitary fancy tasting artichokes, possessing every delicacy, and
resisting cop

Where are they going Wojnarowicz? The doors close in on—
hours. How do you all look tonight?

Will we stroll dreaming of the lost angels of love?
Past crowded brothels and embanked solicitations, home to our
silence?

Ah, dear aunties, glittered beards, lonely old courage teachers, what
angels did you have when Bill O'Reilly quit poling his factor and you
got out on an intermission and stood watching the tweets disappear
on the black waters of Erzulie Freda.

Berkeley Teacher Arrested.

Berkeley, City Of Hookers?

Arrested In Prostitution Case.

Busted For Organizing, Teacher Resigns.

Busted For Prostitution?

**Ohio Teacher,
In Prostitution Sting.**

**Little Rock Teacher
Stings.**

**8 Arrested For Prostitution.
Teacher In Texas?**

**A Springfield Teacher
Busted**

**Cleveland High School
A Teacher**

CITATIONS, AUTOIGNITE

Male, Blond, Blue, 6'2

Was printed on the yellow copy I held, above
INTENTION TO SOLICIT.

It weighed more than paper: our linoleum floor, books,
Purina, rent check, AT&T.

Trent stood up, put his hands onto my wide shoulders while telling
me, you were simply walking home down Hyde Street.

But a girl doesn't get to be
alone and pretty, without selling it. I had

minded my own business that night,
now I held a cite. I couldn't just throw

such papers away. Police and corporations have
rights to the 1st or 14th—personhood, which heels or hoodies

can, or cannot speak of which, Trent said take it to the courthouse and fight. He pulled me in,
exchanged the citation for his hands. Compassion pricks the skin, breaking the sealing
of all our emotional trips. Red

hots and atomic fireballs. I couldn't hear anymore, his
mouth, opened and closed; his hands wrapped around the backs of

my hand. I wondered which backhanded school got me
there. Held by sites of love of law, both clenching. I wanted to bite his flesh

off. Tear his envelope open to get the letter
inside. Cause people that love you have real ultimatums that make you bawl up backbone:

I'll have your back as long as
you respect each piece of your spine-as long as
you keep those pieces on one another so they're strong. So no one can knock you down.
Long as...

the demanding letter would reflect those that came before me: Pink
Threads and hos clamps. The letters would have my back if I kept my marrow.
They'd find me. They'd

replace the citation I held that fined me for WALKING PRETTY
DOWN HYDE STREET like I was Vanguard, like I was a Raging Granny waving it.
Tossing it like I was at Compton's

Cafeteria and it was coffee. Flying out, vaulting our solicitations off before their
faces at 451° Fahrenheit.

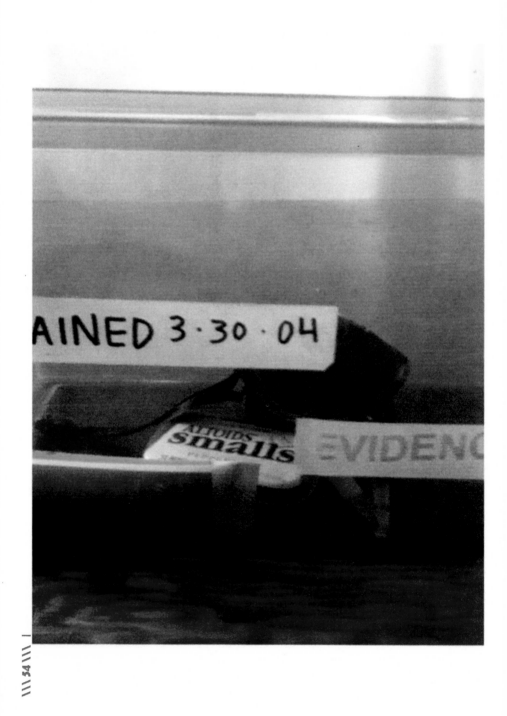

Jerry and I observe the reliefs. Prints-
our test results. We're both typed N,
Courier New font. I'm: T, W, G. I see
Twig; light wood, abilities for fire. Jerry is:
M, W, G. I see MWIG: Mine Warfare
Inspection Group or men penetrating, we're both
negative and in our heads but Jerry's probably thinking, dick. I am,
thinking about the intake counselor; he couldn't imagine my junk. Small, at risk
consider the piece's type: it all becomes
New York Times blood, is part water, flowing through the 70's Times
Square to my SF Soma City Clinic
now, I switched into
health educator: *take my blood. One partner has cum,*
blood, holes and baster, as long as the other has holes to blood
lines I said and his face uh huh'd my body
at risk, consider the parts—my torso
reclined from an L into a \. Jerry will soon turn
a trick so distracted about his penis, blood

type A doesn't care if the O is negative or another type, as long as it
can rush through. As long as it can surge into open lines, the DPH
forms will be out of date cause our shape equals funding after
we are at risk after our elders
dyed, the sheets are still pink from their blood, sweat and head
less men have long dicks. And little dicked men have long
histories, translate
O, trans
gender is a bendable tail
circling around to meet oneself.

Bro, I'm feeling my lips tonight as I stand before you with bony elbows, and confused hips. Bro, you're a ho with a metal mouth and long wooden body that the city woke up last night. You wanted to face shovel the street and extend your limbs out. A flag. I know, hos have fluorescent lights blinking names implying legs and rockets in pockets. My knees are pink with indigo marrow and my clavicles are trying to escape my frame. My front teeth have gotten shy and keep moving to the back of my mouth. You're a man, huh? Do the other dudes feel it in their groin? In their thighs? Cause you know it's not about having it is not about having a front hole bro it's about a found form, one that we can walk into the corner store and feel alright in one that we can fuck in and move with, our iron scent on our hands after peeing and bro, we fear segmentation which is why we're here talking with one another with this silver and black glass. Last night we walked out onto El Paso's Texas Avenue to stretch our legs and saw his truck, bro, and still we came back together in one piece.

Oh subject substitutes, we hear
with you all. Of I, here, hear you
in o, ze, ce, they find sound here
all grey pronouns. They are hearing
you dear, see-er, in sheer third

person, fantastic, part of your
oh I write here, hear ze for u
oh o, I can, write they for your
place O for I, see ce hears
you, hear'r, near. Here we hear.

Service reflect
shun the silent
spaces depicted liminal
houses of offerings,
serve to show mouths,
speaking of hired hands, placing
client tells the pedestals, while workers called to
service one's neighbor, soft
serve a woman manning self
service another our pleasure to
serve and protect, our service
industry, portions of workers serve to show
papers, positioning each body
language, hollering self-honor or petite
size up a gesture, all a personable

touch a fellow face, graciously. It is your
marrow. Our lips

can not get sealed with service
fees and arrest
threats clip our echo.

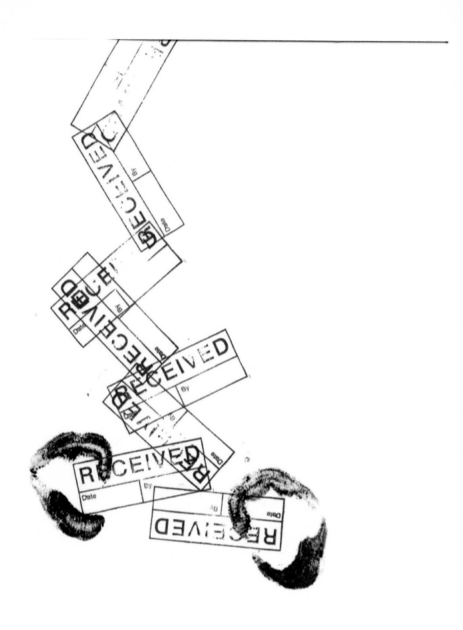

We arrived in North Beach as pom pons. A collection of long strips
tracing to our penises, pussies, purses.

RA RA   RARARARA   RA RA   RARARARA to—
for—your lover you can't see his shirt he tried to give you

the pom pons came out our mouths, homemade film
clips. One large strip stuck out of Mary's mouth. A hard

tongue. The other scenes were skinnier shreds draping from our lower
lips, to chins. A billboard: every job will get their dues

together. Pounding their feet against gravity—
law and frames work thousands of pom pon paper lines bounced

off each other's backs, bumped from one another's lips in 2/4
into for stiffing your lover you can't

see the shirt off his back, we arrived
as pom pons. Leg bouquets with turquoise petals for heels, all dreamt from

hairy holes and hairy broom sticks. The woods switched
the Johns' romantic futures. That one John blew up the bathroom where I disappeared

my hands that were on him, for an affair with a plastic brush. Bristles
stand together, our many arms shook

North Beach, hollering his name,
our balls rattled against

kingpins and pimps. Our glass gauntlets filled his
gaze, that vacant canteena. A barfly slid his long tongue into the barrel of a frothy

pint. Ra Ras catch the maggot's cheek. The cheers pulsed
his lounge walls as LIVE NUDE BOYS, IN
TOWN THIS WEEKEND ONLY, OUT
CALLS ONLY, NO
ATTITUDE the cheerleading props handcrafted from paper, spun
around his dive where bad bosses

hang, their miscellaneous costs tucked under sight. The paper balls fluffed the dead
scene. Said *there's some whores in this*

house and it was bumping off our lips in 2/4 into for stiffing
us lovers you can't steal the shirt off our backs.

Their leather hands open locks and bars, the clasps of each stone
house. The laborers are in front of steel doors that rise to the roof. Openings
holler—monkeys screech, over earth, the backs
bellowing 'still ore! Even after smelting me, even
after me,' walk iron doors out. Hear hands of men paid
under the table. Fingertips lift metal
dowels out of hinge holes. Pings
scatter the surrounding air like Periodical Cicadas,
out, stripped of castings. Unlocking
chains echo a clanging around the brick
buildings. The roars bend to far sides—they circle
faces of these now unbolted museums, and they're almost heard
as scores. Like the inside carvings, dated and named a piece. The hands
flip the awnings
up. Eyelashes snapping
ajar, for gaping at Irises and other flower painted
balls. The help unveils.

POETICS & PROCESS

Thank you Erica Berman, Rosa Alcalá, Benjamin Alire Sáenz, Kevin Killian, Sylvia Aguilar Zéleny, July Oskar Cole, Cleo Woelfle-Erskine, James Share, David Groff, Ammi Keller, Sasha Pimentel, Jay Bessemer, Ruth Oppenheim, Lynne DeSilva-Johnson, and Ezra Nepon for reading this book in its different stages and for your ongoing encouragement and critique of it!

Thank you Pascal Emmer, Carlé Brioso, Sarolta Jane Vay, Qilo Matzen, & Rai Hsu for the sound, visual, or performance collaborations included in, or of which fed, this collection.

Thank you Miss Major, Ralowe Trinitrotoluene Ampu, Mattilda Bernstein Sycamore, Kirk Reed, Laura Agustin, Nalo Hopkinson, Carole Leigh, Nomy Lamm, Michelle Tea, Annie Oakley, Juba Kalamka, for your writing or books that come along with or before this.

The epigraph is taken from Dubravka Ugresic's incredible book, Lend Me Your Character.

ABOUT THE AUTHOR

blake nemec is a writer, teacher and sound/media artist who lives in Chicago. His work has been featured in journals, anthologies, festivals or conferences such as ENTITLE: Undisciplined Environments, *JUPITER 88*, the Red Rover Reading Series, *the Rio Grande Review, Captive Genders; Transembodiment and the Prison Industrial Complex,* or the San Francisco Queer Arts Performance Festival. He received an MFA in bilingual (Spanish and English) poetry/fiction from the University of Texas at El Paso and is a Lambda Literary Fellow. He has long worked as a sound recordist in queer independent movies, the latest being the documentary FREE CeCE!

Collaboration is a potent force his work gushes from, most recently audible in the sound performance project, *Moly B Denim* and the *Social Movements Oral History Project*.

His writing and sound performances work to reveal the extraordinary musicality of everyday conversations by unprotected workers, pansexuals, and gender variant people. He can be reached at: blakej.nemec@gmail.com

Can you introduce yourself, in a way that you would choose?

I feel kin to Cuttlefish. I've always been a hustler. Some of that has been out of a need and some of that has been my adoration of other hustlers. As a homo, transgender, white, ablebodied person who grew up working class, and is the first college graduate in my immediate family, I've needed to reflect on, transform, and ongoingly reimagine the way I move through the world. Writing, health care, art, and independent media communities have been my creative, intellectual, and financial livelihoods for the past twenty-five years; they help me learn how to take care of myself and family, fight the good fight, and make things as discursive tools.

Why are you a poet/writer/artist?

I'm addicted to written excavations. I've found myself returning to writing more than any other creative or intellectual process; it's my longest healthy relationship, so I'm a writer in a literal sense. Reading, writing, and sound experiments are the bewitching corridors through which I enter critical or mindful thinking. Writing has allowed me with few resources, to interpret then express how class, race, gender, ability, or sexuality bends in the U.S. While all art forms can portray phenomena, and stimulate the human senses, literature has the remarkable power to lead people into sensory landscapes while they are simply looking at black and white letters.

What's a "poet" (or "writer" or "artist") anyway? What do you see as your cultural and social role (in the literary / artistic /creative community and beyond)?

As an ESL Instructor for a literacy program in Chicago, my students speak poems in every class when they flip English words to spark a different than intended meaning. A poet intentionally switches the tongue or eyes of the reader. Fiction writers can lead the reader away from self-absorption into another world through quotidian, or experimental, nonformulaic language.

In such art-making processes, every writer should have some tools to bite it. I need to understand myself within the anthropocene and routinely evaluate what writing could be meaningful to readers, or add to discourses.

Talk about the process or instinct to move these poems (or your work in general) as independent entities into a body of work. How and why did this happen? Have you had this intention for a while? What encouraged and/or confounded this (or a book, in general) coming together? Was it a struggle?

The early poems and stories in this collection had unresolved legal, gender, sexuality or race conflicts. Coming out of punk, post-modern, or new narrative influences, I appreciated such undetermined forms. Hence, I wanted to gather them together to view irresolute echoes. Could it make a magnetic whole?

Adoration for the sound of my conversations with other workers, and my activism, inspired the book. While I had ongoing somatic and intellectual resonances from conversations I had with other informal trade workers, it wasn't until my experiences in 2008's Days in April that I formed Bahktinian ideas about writing worker dialogues. I was honored to be invited to and be a part of Days in April, a grassroots response to the de-politicization of May Day. San Francisco Bay Area activists observed that some previous labor rights actions by or during the international workers' day, May Day, had deflated. The group organized with a wide range of informal trade workers to instigate labor rights actions to precede May Day, so that on May 1 a sober economic critique of neoliberalism and U.S. imperialism could occur. As a sex worker activist and former sex worker, I acted as a point person for this worker group. The conversations between the invited sex workers, domestic workers, farm workers, and hotel workers (for example), created social and political alliances as a force against systematic targeting and policing. I will always remember the reiterations of isolation, fear, and uncertainty. At the same time, the tone, pitch and pace of such conversations positively tainted me; unprotected workers talk with a pulse I don't hear between protected workers.

As a Bakhtinian-influenced thinker, I have devotion towards the sounds, and sonic histories, of supposed liminal spaces, of flash intimacies. What can strangers or acquaintances say in passing? Are present bold worker soundscapes akin to the utterances of workers that came before them?

I didn't know if worker vignettes should be sequenced thematically or through form. Many pieces struggled to come alive from my attachments to the theme of unprotected worker conversations. For example, "Two Four Recourse" began as a short story about a series of events called The Blue Hat Special. It was a sex worker activist story where a worker was able to organize against a bad trick. I was holding onto the content, and it wouldn't work in a literary sense. I turned to surrealist or somatics writing exercises; I slept with, cut, braided, or affixed the typed paper onto rotating devices; I observed the rearranged words and tried to put them into an animated form. The section, O, in the book, works to release the collection's theme.

In parallel to my struggles to understand the collection as either theme or form based, I had an overarching narrative question. If the characters, landscapes, and scenarios do not form familiarity, will the reader bond with the text?

I tried to interlace Downton Abbey fan fiction letters into the collection to give it an overarching narrative. A present day maid and butler write a series of love letters to the demonized characters, Thomas Barrow and Ethel Parkins. Eccentric butler and hustler maid pursue a TV crush in order to survive. After several writers told me they didn't know how to relate to the letters, not having my same relationship to Downton Abbey, I scratched them.

Dear Thomas,   09 - 01 - 2013

I was doing some plumbing earlier. The pipes broke and water gushed out of the walls and down the ceiling. I was tending to the scene but it did not seem fast enough and I felt I should help me; the flood wasn't more than one worker could handle alone. I took the wrench and swung it into the metal; a cry for help. Loud echoing rings filled the suite air. I struck again and again until the pipes song split the air. Until the pipes song tore the air open.

I was wrong to ask you to do this for me. I forgot my body is sound.

Yours,
Peter.

What formal structures or other constrictive practices (if any) do you use in the creation of your work?

I used the formal haibun and décima structures for this collection. I had been writing micro-fiction or prose poems but they often felt rigid and unable to exhibit a shiny portrayal of the dialogue or scenario I was reflecting on. I began using the haibun form because the ending haiku works to release the prose tension by untying the narrative. The décima form, with its fixed syllabic and lined meter, gives a nod to the décima worker poems/songs from Spain and Latin America. Décima poems were written to be sung and improvised; everyday dialogues as song can be conceptualized through this form.

Have certain teachers, instructive environments, or readings/writings/work of other creative people informed the way you work/write?

Writers, from Gertrude Stein to Dawn Lundy Martin, emphasize play as a creative fulcrum. I adore this concept and I also generate my favorite work through coltish experimentations. One paradox to this writing process reflects life experiences that led me to Punk or No-Wave writers like Lydia Lunch, or New Narrative writers, Dodie Bellamy, Kevin Killian, or Rober Gluck; I have a nervous and feverish writing process; it is excitable yet disturbed.

I like discipline. Ursula LeGuin's *Steering the Craft* is a writing block go to that reflects the usefulness of syntax discipline. If we were talking about music, I like practicing scales; I like the daily grind.

Jack Spicer talked about dating poetry vs. dating people. I've felt ornery at how spot-on Spicer seems about making a choice between the two, however, when I prioritize one over the other, my writing does blossom or shrivel. Bernadette Myer talks about knowing things, and 'writers don't know things until we put in the long hours of pen to the page.'

Are writers a vessel or can we get some of our guts into the keyboard then the letters? I feel indebted to those before me who explore embodied words, characters who need and have sex, and how somatics relates to language, so Hart Crane, Allen Ginsberg, Samuel Delany, Audre Lorde, David Wojnarowitz, and Aurora Levins-Morales come to mind.

Speaking of monikers, what does your title represent? How was it generated? Talk about the way you titled the book, and how your process of naming (individual pieces, sections, etc) influences you and/or colors your work specifically.

My title comes from a piece in the book with the same title. I wanted to tell the reader the book was about exchanges. So, Sharing Plastic gave me an integral part of the concept. Then, plastic as a rubber, a pliable mode or entity, stood out.

What does this particular work represent to you?

This book is a series of knotty and polyphonic love letters to any worker who fears arrest or demonization. Its de-emphasis, if not exclusion, of the boss/worker power dynamic, requires readers accept, page after page, the power, emotional, gender, sexuality, ability, race, or class sparks between workers themselves. One poem or story excluding the boss is only one sound. One beat has less potential to make readers aware that the typical literary conflict or tension device is absent. I wanted sonic ricochets.

WHY PRINT/DOCUMENT?

The Operating System uses the language "print document" to differentiate from the book-object as part of our mission to distinguish the act of documentation-in-book-FORM from the act of publishing as a backwards-facing replication of the book's agentive *role* as it may have appeared the last several centuries of its history. Ultimately, I approach the book as TECHNOLOGY: one of a variety of printed documents (in this case, bound*) that humans have invented and in turn used to archive and disseminate ideas, beliefs, stories, and other evidence of production.*

Ownership and use of printing presses and access to (or restriction of printed materials) has long been a site of struggle, related in many ways to revolutionary activity and the fight for civil rights and free speech all over the world. While (in many countries) the contemporary quotidian landscape has indeed drastically shifted in its access to platforms for sharing information and in the widespread ability to "publish" digitally, even with extremely limited resources, the importance of publication on physical media has not diminished. In fact, this may be the most critical time in recent history for activist groups, artists, and others to insist upon learning, establishing, and encouraging personal and community documentation practices. Hear me out.

With The OS's print endeavors I wanted to open up a conversation about this: the ultimately radical, transgressive act of creating PRINT /DOCUMENTATION in the digital age. It's a question of the archive, and of history: who gets to tell the story, and what evidence of our life, our behaviors, our experiences are we leaving behind? We can know little to nothing about the future into which we're leaving an unprecedentedly digital document trail — but we can be assured that publications, government agencies, museums, schools, and other institutional powers that be will continue to leave BOTH a digital and print version of their production for the official record. Will we?

As a (rogue) anthropologist and long time academic, I can easily pull up many accounts about how lives, behaviors, experiences — how THE STORY of a time or place — was pieced together using the deep study of correspondence, notebooks, and other physical documents which are no longer the norm in many lives and practices. As we move our creative behaviors towards digital note taking, and even audio and video, what can we predict about future technology that is in any way assuring that our stories will be accurately told – or told at all? How will we leave these things for the record?

In these documents we say:
    WE WERE HERE, WE EXISTED, WE HAVE A DIFFERENT STORY

- Lynne DeSilva-Johnson, Founder/Managing Editor,
THE OPERATING SYSTEM, Brooklyn NY 2017

TITLES IN THE PRINT: DOCUMENT COLLECTION

An Absence So Great and Spontaneous It Is Evidence of Light - Anne Gorrick [2018]
The Book of Everyday Instruction - Chloe Bass [2018]
Executive Orders Book II - a collaboration with the Organism for Poetic Research [2018]
One More Revolution - Andrea Mazzariello [2018]
The Suitcase Tree - Filip Marinovich [2018]
Chlorosis - Michael Flatt and Derrick Mund [2018]
Sussuros a Mi Padre - Erick Sáenz [2018]
Sharing Plastic - Blake Nemec [2018]
The Book of Sounds - Mehdi Navid (Farsi dual language, trans. Tina Rahimi) [2018]
In Corpore Sano : Creative Practice and the Challenged Body [Anthology, 2018];
Lynne DeSilva-Johnson and Jay Besemer, co-editors
Abandoners - Lesley Ann Wheeler [2018]
Jazzercise is a Language - Gabriel Ojeda-Sague [2018]
Death is a Festival - Anis Shivani [2018]
Return Trip / Viaje Al Regreso; Dual Language Edition -
Israel Dominguez,(trans. Margaret Randall) [2018]
Born Again - Ivy Johnson [2018]
Attendance - Rocío Carlos and Rachel McLeod Kaminer [2018
Singing for Nothing - Wally Swist [2018]
Walking Away From Explosions in Slow Motion - Gregory Crosby [2018]
CHAPBOOK SERIES 2018 : Greater Grave - Jacq Greyja; Needles of Itching Feathers -
Jared Schlickling; Want-Catcher - Adra Raine; We, The Monstrous - Mark DuCharme

Lost City Hydrothermal Field - Peter Milne Greiner [2017]
An Exercise in Necromancy - Patrick Roche [Bowery Poetry Imprint, 2017]
Love, Robot - Margaret Rhee[2017]
La Comandante Maya - Rita Valdivia (dual language, trans. Margaret Randall) [2017]
The Furies - William Considine [2017]
Nothing Is Wasted - Shabnam Piryaei [2017]
Mary of the Seas - Joanna C. Valente [2017]
Secret-Telling Bones - Jessica Tyner Mehta [2017]
CHAPBOOK SERIES 2017 : INCANTATIONS
featuring original cover art by Barbara Byers
sp. - Susan Charkes; Radio Poems - Jeffrey Cyphers Wright; Fixing a Witch/Hexing the
Stitch - Jacklyn Janeksela; cosmos a personal voyage by carl sagan ann druyan steven
sotor and me - Connie Mae Oliver
Flower World Variations, Expanded Edition/Reissue - Jerome
Rothenberg and Harold Cohen [2017]
What the Werewolf Told Them / Lo Que Les Dijo El Licantropo -
Chely Lima (trans. Margaret Randall) [2017]
The Color She Gave Gravity - Stephanie Heit [2017]
The Science of Things Familiar - Johnny Damm [Graphic Hybrid, 2017]
agon - Judith Goldman [2017]
To Have Been There Then / Estar Alli Entonces - Gregory Randall
(trans. Margaret Randall) [2017]

Instructions Within - Ashraf Fayadh [2016]
Arabic-English dual language edition; Mona Kareem, translator
Let it Die Hungry - Caits Meissner [2016]
A GUN SHOW - Adam Sliwinski and Lynne DeSilva-Johnson;
So Percussion in Performance with Ain Gordon and Emily Johnson [2016]
Everybody's Automat [2016] - Mark Gurarie
How to Survive the Coming Collapse of Civilization [2016] - Sparrow
CHAPBOOK SERIES 2016: OF SOUND MIND
featuring the quilt drawings of Daphne Taylor
Improper Maps - Alex Crowley; While Listening - Alaina Ferris;
Chords - Peter Longofono; Any Seam or Needlework - Stanford Cheung

TEN FOUR - Poems, Translations, Variations [2015]- Jerome Rothenberg, Ariel
Resnikoff, Mikhl Likht
MARILYN [2015] - Amanda Ngoho Reavey
CHAPBOOK SERIES 2015: OF SYSTEMS OF
featuring original cover art by Emma Steinkraus
Cyclorama - Davy Knittle; The Sensitive Boy Slumber Party Manifesto
- Joseph Cuillier; Neptune Court - Anton Yakovlev; Schema - Anurak Saelow
SAY/MIRROR [2015; 2nd edition 2016] - JP HOWARD
Moons Of Jupiter/Tales From The Schminke Tub [plays, 2014] - Steve Danziger

CHAPBOOK SERIES 2014: BY HAND
Pull, A Ballad - Maryam Parhizkar; Can You See that Sound - Jeff Musillo
Executive Producer Chris Carter - Peter Milne Greiner;
Spooky Action at a Distance - Gregory Crosby;

CHAPBOOK SERIES 2013: WOODBLOCK
featuring original prints from Kevin William Reed
Strange Coherence - Bill Considine; The Sword of Things - Tony Hoffman;
Talk About Man Proof - Lancelot Runge / John Kropa; An Admission as a Warning
Against the Value of Our Conclusions -Alexis Quinlan

DOC U MENT
/däkyəmənt/

First meant "instruction" or "evidence," whether written or not.

noun - a piece of written, printed, or electronic matter that provides
information or evidence or that serves as an official record
verb - record (something) in written, photographic, or other form
synonyms - paper - deed - record - writing - act - instrument

[*Middle English, precept, from Old French, from Latin documentum,
example, proof, from docre, to teach; see dek- in Indo-European roots.*]

Who is responsible for the manufacture of value?

Based on what supercilious ontology have we landed in a space where we vie against other
creative people in vain pursuit of the fleeting credibilities of the scarcity economy,
rather than freely collaborating and sharing openly with each other
in ecstatic celebration of MAKING?

While we understand and acknowledge the economic pressures and fear-mongering
that threatens to dominate and crush the creative impulse,
we also believe that *now more than ever*
we have the tools to relinquish agency via cooperative means,
fueled by the fires of the Open Source Movement.

Looking out across the invisible vistas of that rhizomatic parallel country
we can begin to see our community beyond constraints,
in the place where intention meets
resilient, proactive, collaborative organization.

Here is a document born of that belief, sown purely of imagination and will.
When we document we assert.
We print to make real, to reify our being there.
When we do so with mindful intention to address our process,
to open our work to others, to create beauty in words in space,
to respect and acknowledge the strength of the page we now hold physical,
a thing in our hand… we remind ourselves that, like Dorothy:
we had the power all along, my dears.

THE PRINT! DOCUMENT SERIES
is a project of
the trouble with bartleby
in collaboration with
the operating system